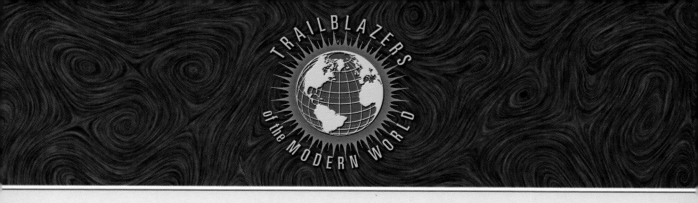

MARGARET MEAD

By Geoffrey M. Horn

WORLD ALMANAC® LIBRARY

Please visit our web site at: www.worldalmanaclibrary.com
For a free color catalog describing World Almanac® Library's list
of high-quality books and multimedia programs, call 1-800-848-2928 (USA)
or 1-800-387-3178 (Canada). World Almanac® Library's fax: (414) 332-3567.

Library of Congress Cataloging-in-Publication Data available upon request from publisher.
Fax (414) 336-0157 for the attention of the Publishing Records Department.

ISBN 0-8368-5099-8 (lib. bdg.)
ISBN 0-8368-5259-1 (softcover)

First published in 2004 by
World Almanac® Library
330 West Olive Street, Suite 100
Milwaukee, WI 53212 USA

Copyright © 2004 by World Almanac® Library.

Project manager: Jonny Brown
Editor: Alan Wachtel
Design and page production: Scott M. Krall
Photo research: Diane Laska-Swanke
Indexer: Walter Kronenberg

Photo credits: © AP/Wide World Photos: 38, 42 bottom; © Bettmann/CORBIS: 4, 9, 10, 12, 13, 14, 19, 22, 23, 27, 29, 30 top, 32, 34 both, 37, 40, 41, 42 top; © Paula Bronstein/Getty Images: 7; © Jack Fields/CORBIS: 26, 30 bottom; © FPG/Getty Images: cover; © Bob Gomel/Time Life Pictures/Getty Images: 36; © Dallas and John Heaton/CORBIS: 33 top; © Hulton Archive/Getty Images: 8, 21, 33 bottom; © Wolfgang Kaehler/CORBIS: 6, 31; Scott M. Krall/© World Almanac Library, 2004: 25 all; © Steve Liss/Time Life Pictures/Getty Images: 35; © John Loengard/Time Life Pictures/Getty Images: 39; © Lee Snider; Lee Snider/CORBIS: 20

Printed in the United States of America

1 2 3 4 5 6 7 8 9 08 07 06 05 04

TABLE of CONTENTS

Words that appear in the glossary are printed in **boldface**
type the first time they occur in the text.

CHAPTER 1

EXPLORING NEW WORLDS

In this 1934 photo, Mead displays some of the "trophy heads" she collected in New Guinea while studying three Pacific Island peoples.

"To explore strange new worlds . . . to seek out new life and new civilizations . . . to boldly go where no man has gone before." With these words, the creators of the *Star Trek* television series in the mid-1960s described the mission of the starship *Enterprise*. There was nothing particularly new about this idea. Margaret Mead had been doing it for decades.

Of course, when the authors of *Star Trek* described the culture, customs, rituals, and language of the Klingons or some other made-up species, they could let their imaginations run wild. Mead, on the other hand, was not a science fiction writer but a **social scientist**—a scholar who studies human societies in a clear-headed and factual way. She lived for months or years among each of the Pacific Island peoples about whom she wrote. She wrote down almost everything she saw and heard. She took thousands of photographs to make sure she had an accurate record of her observations.

Mead was a pioneer in the field of **anthropology**—a science that focuses on the similarities and differences between groups of human beings. Beneath the skin, human beings are pretty much alike in their basic biology. Every normally equipped woman or man has a brain, a heart, blood, bones, muscles, and organs for seeing, touching, smelling, hearing, breathing, eating, feeling pain and pleasure, and having sex.

Despite their similar biology, however, human beings show enormous differences in their culture and customs. For example, in the United States, many parents push their babies in carriages or strollers. In New Guinea, on the other hand, Mead saw women carry their infants in baskets suspended from their foreheads.

People speak many hundreds of different languages. Music, dance, clothing, housing, dating and mating practices, how people celebrate holidays, and how they bury their dead—all these show great variety from one culture to another. What could we learn, Mead wanted to know, by studying people whose cultures were very different from our own?

TO SAMOA AND BEYOND

Mead was only twenty-three years old when she made her first voyage to the South Pacific in 1925. "I had all the courage of almost complete ignorance," she later wrote. "I had read everything that had been written about the Pacific Island peoples. . . . But I myself had never been abroad or on a ship, had never spoken a foreign language or stayed in a hotel by myself. In fact, I had never spent a day in my life alone."

The book that emerged from her first Pacific voyage was *Coming of Age in Samoa*. First published in 1928, the book was an immediate best-seller. One reason for its popularity was that the book was beautifully written, in a style that people who were not scholars could understand. Another reason for its enormous influence

What Anthropologists Do

An anthropologist is a scientist who studies the origins, behavior, and development of human beings. The word "anthropology" comes from two Greek roots: *anthropo-*, which means "human," and *-logy*, meaning "knowledge." There are two major branches of anthropology: physical anthropology and cultural anthropology.

Physical anthropology deals with how human beings have evolved and adapted to cope with their physical surroundings. Physical anthropologists study the bones, tools, and other remains of people who lived thousands or even millions of years ago. By studying skeletons of some of our ancient human ancestors, for example, a physical anthropologist can tell whether they walked upright or moved on all fours.

Cultural anthropology emphasizes close observation of language, culture, and customs in order to show how different societies develop. For example, cultural anthropologists have studied groups as different as the Inuit in the Arctic, the Sioux Indians of South Dakota, and Italian families in New Jersey.

How women in New Guinea hold, feed, and teach their children is the sort of subject that cultural anthropologists study.

was that it described, in glowing terms, a culture whose view of sex was much freer than that of most Americans and Europeans. Mead did not shrink from suggesting that the "primitive" Samoans appeared to have a healthier attitude toward their own bodies than did the more "civilized" peoples of the English-speaking world. This message took on renewed power during the "sexual revolution" of the 1960s.

On Bali, Indonesia, an eleven-year-old girl performs a dance at a show for tourists in 2002. Mead studied the traditional culture of Bali while living on the island in the 1930s.

Watch Your Language!

Like most Americans of her time, Margaret Mead called some peoples of the Pacific Islands "primitives" or "savages." Today, scholars go to great lengths to avoid using such terms, which sound like insults. For example, instead of talking about a "primitive society," a scholar might refer to an "isolated culture." Rather than describing people who live in the United States as "modern" or "civilized," anthropologists prefer to use a phrase like "urban, industrialized societies."

Again and again throughout her long career, Mead took up the question of how cultures assigned different roles to men and women. She did not deny that some differences between women and men were based on biology. For example, only women can become pregnant, give birth, and produce breast milk for their children. But in most cases, she concluded, the female and male roles were based solely on culture and custom, not biology or instinct. The recognition that many views about men and women came from old habits, outmoded ideas, or sexist stereotypes gave a major boost to the women's rights movement.

This photo of Mead was taken in 1928, when her book *Coming of Age in Samoa* became a best-seller.

AN INDEPENDENT WOMAN

Many supporters of women's rights looked to Mead as a model of what a strong-minded, independent woman could accomplish. She kept her own name when she got married in 1923—a decision much less common in those days than it is today. She was married three times, and each marriage ended in divorce. "I've never wanted to belong to another person," she said, "nor would I ever want anyone to belong to me."

Mead became one of the world's best-known social scientists at a time when female professors at major universities were still a rarity. She published three dozen books, wrote many hun-

In Her Own Words—Margaret Mead on Anthropology

In the following passage from her book *Blackberry Winter: My Earlier Years* (1972), Mead challenges social scientists to find ways to help "primitive" peoples survive and thrive in the modern world. She also complains about some anthropologists who seem to forget that the people they are studying are human beings. For example, some social scientists spend more time analyzing statistics on their computers than actually observing how real people behave. Other groups make different kinds of errors:

There are those rebels in search of a "natural" life, who would like to try the experiment of living in the midst of some primitive group. There are the sentimentalists who would like to put fences around the remaining groups of primitive peoples and treat them like wild creatures in a game preserve. And, increasingly, there are those who are attempting to turn primitive peoples, living on the edge of modern civilization, into tourist attractions—as if they were exotic animals set out for public view in a zoo. But how many social scientists are there, today, who are trying to think out ways in which primitive peoples, where they still exist, can become our partners and co-workers in the search for knowledge that may, in the end, save their children and ours?

dreds of articles, and regularly gave more than a hundred lectures a year. During the last decades of her life, she wrote a monthly column for *Redbook*, where her views on current topics reached a wide general audience.

For much of her adult life she worked for the American Museum of Natural History, in New York City. She was hired in 1926 as a **curator**, and her job was to help assemble the museum's Pacific Island collection. Later the museum listed her as an expert on a large number of different subjects, including family life, mental health, how countries deal with each other, and how societies change.

In 1976, Mead celebrated both her seventy-fifth birthday and her fiftieth year of working as a curator at the American Museum of Natural History.

CHAPTER 2

"IT'S A PITY YOU AREN'T A BOY"

Margaret Mead was born at West Park Hospital in Philadelphia, Pennsylvania, on December 16, 1901. She was the oldest child of Edward Sherwood Mead, an **economist** at the University of Pennsylvania, and Emily Fogg Mead, a social researcher and reformer. They had met in Illinois, while both were students at the University of Chicago, and had married in the summer of 1900.

Edward made no secret of the fact that he had hoped his firstborn would be a son. "It's a pity you aren't a boy," he told the young Margaret. "You'd have gone far." Emily delivered a boy child, Richard, in 1904, when Margaret was two years old. A third child, Katherine, died in infancy. Later the Meads had two more daughters: Elizabeth, born in 1909, and Priscilla, born in 1911.

Margaret's parents met in Chicago, shown here in this early twentieth-century street scene.

A Scar on the Family

Katherine's death in March 1907, at the age of nine months, caused a wound from which the Mead family never fully recovered. Remarkably, Margaret had been allowed to name Katherine, and she felt particularly close to her baby sister. For years, her "lost little sister" lived on in her daydreams. Margaret believed Katherine's death also deeply wounded her father, who showed much less affection to Elizabeth and Priscilla, the two children born after Katherine.

"THE ORIGINAL PUNK" AND HER PARENTS

Margaret's father called her "Punk" until Richard was born, after which he called Margaret "the original punk" and Richard the "boy-punk." Edward, who stood six feet tall, called the much shorter Emily his "Tiny Wife." By all accounts, Edward was neither a particularly loving father to his children nor a faithful husband to his wife. In her book *Blackberry Winter*, Margaret recalled his rough touch:

> *He was awkward in his handling of his children, and his determined touch hurt. I have many memories of this—of having my shoes put on the wrong feet the morning my brother was born, of being held too tightly, of once having my hair brushed too vigorously.*

Margaret wrote that her father "did not trust his own body" and had an "enormous amount" of physical fear. This anxiety led him to discourage his children from riding bicycles. He also barred his children from horseback riding after Margaret and Richard had a "minor mishap" in which they fell off a horse.

Later in life, Margaret connected her father's physical fear with the fact that her grandfather, Giles Mead, had passed away before the age of forty. Edward was only six years old when he watched his father die of pneumonia. Margaret also believed that a gun-related incident in which one student had nearly killed another had left her father with a lifelong fear of physical violence.

While Margaret was growing up, American women took to the streets to demand the right to vote.

Margaret had much fonder memories of her mother, from whom she got her short stature—when fully grown, Margaret stood only five feet two inches tall—and her zeal for social causes. "For all her slightness and delicate beauty," she wrote, "my mother had been a determined and **impetuous** young girl." Emily told her children that when Grover Cleveland, a Democrat, was elected president in 1884, she led all her classmates out into the streets of Chicago to celebrate.

Emily felt strongly that American society needed to treat poor people, women, and African Americans more fairly. She felt uncomfortable receiving presents, because she always thought the money would have been better spent on some worthy social cause. She was an ardent supporter of the American Association of University Women, which worked to improve opportunities for female students and teachers in higher education.

Margaret warmly remembered her mother's "radiant smile," her unfailing generosity, and her trustworthiness and dependability. But in her mother, too,

Like Mother, Like Daughter

Like her daughter, Emily Fogg Mead was a social scientist. Emily's major project was to study the Italian immigrant families who had settled in Hammonton, New Jersey. Hammonton is located in the southern part of the state, about midway between Philadelphia and Atlantic City. The Mead family lived there for a while, and Margaret—not yet a teenager—helped her mother with her research.

Often they would go to weddings to observe how the Italian families behaved. "Most of the women were dabbing tears out of their eyes," Margaret said later. "My mother was always busy taking notes. She taught me not only how to go, but what to look for."

Margaret used her knowledge of Italian immigrant culture when she was a graduate student at Columbia University in the 1920s. Her research project for her master's degree was titled *Intelligence Tests of Italian and American Children*.

Margaret with her mother, Emily Fogg Mead, in 1905

Margaret realized something was lacking. "She had no gift for play," Mead later wrote, "and very little for pleasure or comfort."

IN THE COMPANY OF WOMEN

Edward Mead's work took him to many different towns, and the Mead family moved often. By the time she reached her teens, Margaret estimated that her family had lived in sixty different houses. Because her father was often away on business, the child-rearing duties fell largely to Emily and to Edward's mother, Martha Adaline Mead.

Mead, who thought deeply about the importance of family life, wrote the text for a book of photographs called *Family* in 1965.

Martha and Giles Mead had married after the **Civil War**. She and Giles were schoolteachers. They went to college together, graduated on the same day, and became active as school reformers. Eventually, he became a school superintendent, and she became a school principal. Widowed when Giles died in 1880, Martha lived with her son and daughter-in-law from the time they married until her own death in 1927.

Emily was not thrilled to have Martha living with her, but as a dutiful daughter-in-law, she made sure that, wherever the family was living, Martha always got the best room. When the family moved to a farm during Margaret's preteen years, the children were told they were living there "because Grandma believed every child had a right to grow up on a farm."

Margaret went to kindergarten and to high school, but was home-schooled during most of the in-between years. Lessons at home from her grandmother rarely took more than an hour a day. That gave Margaret plenty of opportunities to read, run, get into mischief, and spend time with her younger brother, who was as sickly as Margaret was vigorous.

Memorizing facts played little part in the lessons her grandmother taught her. "I learned to observe the world around me and to note what I saw—to observe flowers and children and baby chicks," Mead wrote later. "She taught me to read for the sense of what I read and to enjoy learning."

In Her Own Words—Margaret Mead on Her Grandmother

In *Blackberry Winter*, Mead devoted an entire chapter to her relationship with her grandmother Martha. Mead pointed out that because both her mother and her grandmother had careers, she never had any "reason to doubt that brains were suitable in a woman." In the following passage, Margaret reflects on other lessons she learned from her mother and grandmother.

I think it was my grandmother who gave me my ease in being a woman. She was unquestionably feminine—small and dainty and pretty. . . . She had gone to college when this was a very unusual thing for a girl to do, she had a firm grasp of anything she paid attention to, she had married and had a child, and she had a career of her own. . . .

The content of my conscience came from my mother's concerns for other people and the state of the world and from my father's insistence that the only thing worth doing is to add to the store of exactly known facts. But the strength of my conscience came from Grandma, who meant what she said. Perhaps nothing is more valuable for a child than living with an adult who is firm and loving—and Grandma was loving. I loved the feel of her soft skin, but she would never let me give her an extra kiss when I said good night.

COMING OF AGE

The onset of **adolescence** brought many changes in Margaret Mead. When she was eleven years old, her body began to mature. She was told that she should stop playing baseball and other "vigorous games," but she went on playing them anyway.

Margaret was developing spiritually as well as physically. Neither of her parents were churchgoers, and her grandmother, a Methodist, had stopped attending services when Margaret was very young. To her parents' surprise, Mead started going to Quaker meetings regularly. Within a few years, her faith had found an anchor in the Episcopal Church. "I enjoyed prayer, I enjoyed church," she wrote later. "The other children I knew thought all of this was odd. They went to church when they were told to do so, and they rolled pennies in their hats or pinched each other during the sermon."

A Question of Belief

Mead took her commitment to the Episcopal Church very seriously. During the 1960s, she was asked to serve on a committee to revise the Book of Common Prayer, the official prayer book of the Church of England and of the Episcopal Church in the United States. She met regularly in New York City with other members of the panel, which included some distinguished church leaders.

One day the panel was discussing the biblical story of Noah's flood. Other peoples have also recounted stories of a disastrous flood that happened in ancient times.

Mead listened intently as one of the bishops expressed his doubts. "Nobody believes that in this day and age," he said. "Bishops may not," Mead answered, "but anthropologists do."

SCHOOL DAYS

Margaret spent her teen years in various towns in eastern Pennsylvania. First she attended the Buckingham Friends School at Lahaska, then a public high school in Doylestown, and finally the Holmquist School, a private academy in the middle of an artists' colony at New Hope. To all appearances, she was a happy, outgoing girl. More often than not, if the school had a play, dance, party, or competition, she was the one who organized it. On top of all that, she carried a heavy burden of household chores, which included helping to care for her two younger sisters.

Inwardly, however, she felt a need for new and greater challenges. She began to keep a diary, wrote poetry and plays, launched a school magazine, and started writing a novel. She began to think about what she wanted to do with her life. The experiences of her mother and grandmother taught her that it was possible, though not easy, to have a career and be a wife and mother. She did not yet know which career she wanted—perhaps a lawyer or writer, she thought— but she was certain she would pursue a profession.

Something else she decided was that when she married she would not take her husband's name. "I'm going to be famous someday," she told her father when she was in her early twenties, "and I'm going to be known by my own name!"

MEAD'S "STUDENT MARRIAGE"

In June 1917, when she was still six months short of her sixteenth birthday, Margaret met Luther Sheeleigh Cressman. Luther, who was twenty years old and studying Greek and Latin at Penn State, was the younger brother of a science teacher at Doylestown High School. Margaret described him as "tall and slender and well built." He read and wrote poetry, was as adept at shooting with a camera as with a gun, was a splendid dancer, and "had an engaging grin and a wry sense of humor."

They saw each other several times during the autumn, and by Christmas 1917, they were engaged. Luther described the starlit night when they declared their feelings for each other.

We had not been talking much, but as we walked some subtle communication had been going on between us. We stopped, turned facing each other, and when I told her I loved her she replied, "I love you, too." She lifted her veil, worn against the cold, and our words were sealed with our kiss.

Luther was studying to be a minister and, for a while, Margaret took comfort in the thought of becoming "a minister's wife with six children." They married six years later (in *Blackberry Winter*, Mead called it her "student marriage"). By then, however, Margaret's life had taken several startling new directions.

The Shoes Lasted a Lot Longer Than the Marriage

For reasons discussed in the next two chapters, Margaret and Luther's marriage did not last very long. He left the ministry, became a teacher and social scientist, and eventually headed the Department of Anthropology at the University of Oregon in Eugene.

During the late 1930s, Cressman and his students were exploring Fort Rock Cave in eastern Oregon when they came upon a large collection of sandals woven from shredded sagebrush bark. Scientific testing showed that one of the sandals was more than 9,300 years old. In the 1980s, the Nike athletic shoe company put out a poster that called Cressman's discovery "Oregon's oldest running shoes." The sandals are now displayed at the University of Oregon's Museum of Natural History, which Cressman founded in 1936.

BARNARD, BOAS, AND BENEDICT

Margaret had expected to enroll in the autumn of 1919 at Wellesley, a women's college near Boston, Massachusetts, that her mother had attended for a while. In the spring of 1919, however, her father suffered some financial setbacks, and he soured on the idea of Margaret's attending college at all. Emily rescued Margaret's college plans by persuading Edward that their daughter should attend DePauw—the same Indiana university where he had studied about twenty-five years earlier.

Margaret spent only a year at DePauw. She enjoyed the classes and respected her professors but was treated as an outsider by most of her fellow students. At DePauw, her unusual upbringing, her East Coast accent, the clothes she wore, the way she decorated her dorm room, even the fact that she did not chew gum all were counted against her.

After suffering through the year in Indiana, Margaret persuaded her father to allow her to transfer to Barnard College. Barnard was located near and was associated with Columbia University in New York City. For Margaret, now nineteen years old, New York City had everything that Indiana lacked—great poets, great artists, great theater, and, not so coincidentally, her **fiancé**, Luther Cressman.

At Barnard, Margaret found the social acceptance

New York City was one of the world's great centers of art, theater, literature, and learning in the 1920s, just as it is today.

that had eluded her at DePauw. She quickly bonded with a small group of bright, talented female students who all shared an apartment on West 116th Street. The group members called themselves the Ash Can Cats. The name was given to them by a favorite drama professor, who chided them for their imperfect grooming by saying, "You girls who sit up all night readin' poetry come to class lookin' like Ash Can Cats." Many of the Ash Can Cats remained Margaret's friends for life.

FRANZ BOAS

Margaret entered her senior year at Barnard in the fall of 1922. Seniors were allowed to choose among the college's most outstanding offerings. Mead chose a course in anthropology given by Franz Boas. The decision changed her life.

Born in Germany in 1858, Boas had mastered physics, mathematics, and geography before becoming a professor of anthropology at Columbia University in 1899. At first, he had believed that the culture of a people was determined mainly by geography and climate— how cold it was, how much it rained or snowed, how much food could be grown, and so forth. But his careful study of the Inuit people who lived on Baffin Island, an Arctic region that is part of Canada, had convinced him that this was wrong. He decided that a people's culture and customs were based not on biology or on certain inborn racial traits but on traditions that may or may not be passed down from one generation to the next.

A recent photo of Barnard College, where Mead first studied anthropology with Franz Boas and Ruth Benedict

Nature Versus Nurture

The disagreement over whether biology or culture plays a greater part in determining how people behave is sometimes called the "nature versus nurture" debate. People who believe that biology and instinct are more important are said to favor the "nature" side of the debate. People who think social and cultural factors are more important are said to favor the "nurture" side.

This debate applies to many different kinds of scientific questions. Is musical talent a gift that some people are born with or a skill that parents can develop in their children? Do people become addicts because their bodies crave the chemicals in drugs or alcoholic drinks or because they grew up in troubled homes or bad neighborhoods? Most scientists believe that both nature and nurture affect the way people behave.

At the time, many educated people believed that some races were "purer" or more highly evolved than others. Some white Americans had used this theory to justify taking blacks as slaves. Later, Adolf Hitler would proclaim the idea that Germans were a "master race" who had the duty to kill millions of people Hitler claimed were inferior. Boas flatly rejected such racist attitudes. He thought no race was innately superior to any other.

Hitler and the Nazis believed in the idea of a "master race"—an idea totally rejected by Boas.

Before Boas, most anthropologists spent little time living among the people they wrote about. Instead, they relied on travelers' colorful accounts of "primitive" cultures. Boas taught that anthropologists should commit themselves to getting to know different peoples, observing their customs, learning their languages, and making detailed reports about everything they observed. Only through such **fieldwork**, he argued, could anthropology become a true science.

Although he was a stern and demanding teacher, Boas proved to be an excellent **mentor** for Mead. His intellectual standards were very high. He knew and encouraged many of the world's most brilliant scholars. And, more than many professors at that time, he felt comfortable working with women.

Franz Boas in 1906

In Her Own Words— Margaret Mead on Franz Boas

Mead shows her keen eye in this sharp portrait of her mentor Franz Boas, as she knew him at Columbia in the 1920s. He continued teaching until 1937 and died in 1942.

Boas was a surprising and somewhat frightening teacher. He had a bad side and a good side of his face. On one side there was a long dueling scar from his student days in Germany— an unusual pursuit for a Jewish student—on which his eyelid drooped and teared from a recent stroke. But seen from the other side, his face showed him to be as handsome as he had been as a young man.

RUTH BENEDICT

When Mead enrolled in Franz Boas's anthropology course in the fall of 1922, his teaching assistant was a graduate student named Ruth Benedict. Margaret was twenty years old, and Ruth was thirty-five. Their friendship, which lasted until Ruth's death in 1948, played a central role in both their lives.

Born in 1887 in New York City, Ruth Fulton Benedict was a bright but troubled girl, with a terrible temper. Her father died when she was two years old—a family calamity that haunted her through her entire life. Adding to her feelings of isolation was the fact that a case of measles at an early age had made her partially deaf.

Benedict did not choose anthropology as a career until she was already in her thirties. She did her fieldwork among the Indians of the Southwest. Benedict was convinced that Native American cultures were changing rapidly and that the elders who knew the old ways would not be around much longer. The clock was ticking. Anyone who wanted to get an accurate picture of the history of the first Americans would need to study them while the elders were still alive.

At lunch in the spring of 1923, Ruth talked with Margaret about the younger woman's career plans. Margaret still was not sure she wanted to make anthropology her profession.

Ruth Benedict in her later years

In Her Own Words— Margaret Mead on Ruth Benedict

This passage, which comes from Mead's 1974 book about Benedict, describes what Ruth was like when Margaret and her classmates first met her in the early 1920s.

We saw her as a very shy . . . middle-aged woman whose fine, mouse-colored hair never stayed quite pinned up. Week after week she wore . . . the same drab dress. Men wore the same clothes every day, she said. Why shouldn't a woman, also? She stammered a little when she talked with us and sometimes blushed scarlet. . . .

In spite of her shyness, Ruth Benedict's enthusiasm for the anthropological world she had so recently entered . . . captivated all of us.

For one thing, the financial rewards were uncertain. "Professor Boas and I have nothing to offer but an opportunity to do work that matters," Ruth told her. That was all Margaret needed to hear.

To this day, Benedict's name is linked with Mead's among the founders of cultural anthropology. In 1934, Benedict published her masterwork, *Patterns of Culture*. In that book, she argued that cultures took many forms. What was perfectly normal in one culture, she said, might be abnormal in another and vice versa. The book was tremendously influential. Like Mead's *Coming of Age in Samoa*, it suggested that people should spend less time judging each other and more time trying to understand each other.

Revealing a Secret

Six years after Margaret Mead's death, her only child, Mary Catherine Bateson, published a book called *With a Daughter's Eye*. In her book, Bateson—also an anthropologist—wrote that Margaret Mead and Ruth Benedict had been lovers as well as coworkers and friends.

Bateson wrote that she had decided to reveal her mother's secret so that people could have a clearer and more honest understanding of Mead's work. Such honesty was particularly important because Mead's writings had helped to shape public attitudes about love and sex.

"Margaret," her daughter wrote, "continued throughout her life to affirm the possibility of many kinds of love, with both men and women, rejecting neither."

Facing page: Mead traveled many thousands of miles during the 1920s and 1930s, to the island regions now known as Indonesia, Papua New Guinea, and American Samoa. After each of her ocean voyages to the South Pacific, she returned home to the eastern United States, visiting many other places along the way.

VOYAGES OF DISCOVERY

Margaret Mead did the work for which she is most famous—her studies of the peoples of the Pacific Islands—during the 1920s and 1930s. The first of these voyages, to the territory now known as American Samoa, took place in the mid-1920s. Boas had wanted her to study Native American cultures, just as he and Benedict were doing. But Mead was fascinated with the cultures of **Polynesia**, a broad region of the Pacific Ocean extending all the way from Hawaii to New Zealand. Boas warned her that this might be dangerous. Some young male researchers had been killed or had fallen fatally ill while working in such remote areas. Mead, however, insisted that she wanted to work in the South Pacific.

On one important question, however, she was willing to compromise. She wanted to study cultural change. Boas wanted her to study

Walking with a Light Step

Many writers have commented that Margaret—small, young, and female—resembled in some ways the adolescent girls she was studying. Mead did not reject the comparison. She wrote that in her twenties she "walked with a light step, the light step of a small, determined eleven-year-old, with no weight on my shoulders."

Sheltered by densely wooded hills, Pago Pago harbor remains an important port of call for oceangoing vessels in the South Pacific.

adolescent girls. The questions she set out to answer in her research tried to satisfy both requirements. Do adolescents in other cultures have the same kinds of serious problems that many American teenagers experience? If not, why not? If American society is to blame, how can we change it to make the early teen years less difficult?

SAMOAN JOURNEY

The S.S. *Sonoma* steamed into Pago Pago harbor, on the island of Tutuila, on August 31, 1925, beginning Margaret Mead's nine-month stay in Samoa. Much of that time she spent on the island of Ta'u, interacting with an endless stream of Samoan children—boys as well as girls—who visited her at most hours of the day and night and called her *Makelita*. She learned the Samoan language and talked with dozens of girls about their hopes, their plans, their emotional and physical experiences, and their relationships with other girls, with boys, and with their families.

Although she greatly enjoyed the time she spent with these children, she also kept a certain distance between the Samoans' lives and her own. In October, while she was still on Tutuila, she wrote to Boas explaining why she had chosen to live with a white family instead of a Samoan family. In particular, she was not fond of Samoan food and worried about its effects on her health. She also wanted to avoid "the nerve-wracking conditions of living with half a dozen people in the same room, in a house without walls, always sitting on the floor and sleeping in constant expectation of having a pig or a chicken thrust itself upon one's notice."

Mead concluded from her fieldwork that adolescent girls in Samoa lived much less stressful lives than girls in the United States. This was not because of any biological differences between Samoan girls and American girls. No, Mead thought, the difference in stress level had to come from differences in culture. "Samoa knows but one way of life and teaches it to her children," Mead wrote. She contrasted Samoan culture with American society, which she viewed as bombarding children with all kinds of conflicting messages and standards: about work, about money, about their bodies, about sex. No wonder adolescence in the United States was so often a time of turmoil!

Mead wrote *Coming of Age in Samoa* in the mid-1920s, and the book came out in 1928. The published book was different from her original version because the publisher, the William Morrow Company, asked her to clarify what the United States should do to relieve the pressure on young Americans. In the revised text, she urged schools and teachers to train American young people how to make wise choices. She also urged parents to avoid forcing their own religious beliefs on their chil-

Mead not only studied the peoples of the South Pacific—she also collected their fabrics and artwork for the American Museum of Natural History.

dren. Instead, she wrote, children must be allowed to develop healthy bodies and minds free of prejudice and narrow-mindedness.

"Children must be taught how to think, not what to think," she urged. "They must be taught that many ways are open to them," and that they have the right to choose which path to follow.

Firestorm Over Freeman

In 1983, Derek Freeman, an Australian anthropologist, published a book called *Margaret Mead and Samoa: The Making and Unmaking of an Anthropological Myth*. Freeman attacked Mead's earlier book, charging that her knowledge of the Samoan language was poor, her research was sloppy, and her ideas about Samoan society were wrong. Freeman later charged that Mead had been the victim of a huge hoax. When asked about sex, he claimed, the Samoan girls had been so embarrassed they teased her by making up phony answers.

Publication of Freeman's book ignited a firestorm of argument that continues to this day. His angry tone and relentless criticism of Mead's life and work offended many of her admirers, but Freeman was a recognized scholar, with many years of experience in Samoa, so his charges could not be easily dismissed.

One side effect of what has become known as the Mead-Freeman controversy is that teachers and students have taken a fresh look at Mead's writings. Because Freeman's criticism helped keep her name alive, book sales of *Coming of Age in Samoa* have actually gone up in recent decades.

During the summer of 1926, Mead set sail from Pago Pago to Sydney, Australia. There, she boarded the S.S. *Chitral*, which was making its maiden voyage to England. She was still married to Luther Cressman, and after almost a year in the South Pacific she was looking forward to reuniting with him in London.

Also on board the *Chitral* was a New Zealander named Reo Franklin Fortune. He was tall, good-looking, intense, and, as Margaret soon found out, as jealous as he was smart. They were immediately attracted to each other. By the time the *Chitral* reached Europe, she knew her marriage to Luther was over. Margaret and Luther were divorced in 1928, the same year she married Reo.

Unlike Luther, Reo was prepared to travel with Margaret to the South Pacific. Their first field trip together was to the village of Peré, on the island of Manus. Manus was part of the Admiralty Islands, a group of about eighteen islands that now belong to the nation of Papua New Guinea. On Manus, Mead studied the mental development of young children. They called her *Piyap*— the "Woman of the West"—and were happy to draw for her some 35,000 pieces of art, all of which she saved. From her fieldwork in Manus she produced a book for general readers, *Growing Up in New Guinea* (1930), as well as a scientific book on Admiralty Islands family structure for other anthropologists.

Margaret in 1928— a heady year for the young anthropologist

Mead examines a model of a Manus lagoon village. "The streets are waterways, the houses set on high posts over the water," she wrote. "All life is conducted by means of canoes."

A Samoan chief in traditional costume, photographed in the mid-1960s

Reo also accompanied Margaret on another trip to the New Guinea region in the early 1930s. On this trip, she studied what women and men were like among three very different peoples: the Arapesh, the Mundugumor, and the Tchambuli. She observed that among the Arapesh, both men and women were gentle and helpful. Among the Mundugumor, on the other hand, both men and women tended to be violent, jealous, and aggressive. (Margaret did not like the Mundugumor and thought they brought out the worst parts of Reo's personality.) In the third group, the Tchambuli, men did not show the same traits as women. Instead, the women seemed more dominant and the men more dependent.

Mead brought these observations together in *Sex and Temperament in Three Primitive Societies* (1935), one of her most important books. She concluded from her research that the cultural meanings of "man" and "woman" were not set in stone. The biology of Arapesh, Mundugumor, Tchambuli, and American men and women was exactly the same. But the roles the four societies assigned to men and women were very different.

Her research provided powerful evidence for defenders of women's rights in the United States. The idea that men should dominate women on the job or at home wasn't "natural" at all, they said; it was just a bias built into American culture. If women and men could be more equal in Arapesh, they reasoned, then women and men could also be more equal in the United States.

Traditional and modern houses stand side-by-side in the Tingwon island group, part of Papua New Guinea.

CHAPTER 6

THE YEARS WITH BATESON

Life among the violent Mundugumor of New Guinea had shown Margaret Mead the darker side of Reo Fortune. She was prepared to feel charmed in December 1932 when she and Reo left the Mundugumor and met an English anthropologist named Gregory Bateson. Tall, gangly, and immensely likable, Bateson struck a chord with the weary Margaret by saying, at their first meeting, "You're tired," and offering her a chair. "I sank into it," wrote Mead, "feeling that these were the first cherishing words I had heard from anyone in all the Mundugumor months." Mead was further charmed when Bateson pulled out a copy of her book *Growing Up in New Guinea* and began questioning her about her research.

Margaret, Reo, and Gregory quickly became friends, but it was not long before Fortune began to feel that his wife and Bateson were turning into a twosome. Feelings of jealousy brought out Reo's violent streak, and it was soon obvious that their marriage was falling apart. In 1935, Mead divorced Fortune, and the following year she and Bateson got married in Singapore. Just as Reo and Margaret had launched their marriage with a field trip to Manus in 1928, so Margaret and her third husband made a beeline for Bali, in what is now Indonesia. In 1936, they began a

Mead had been doing fieldwork among the peoples of New Guinea for more than a year when she returned home to New York City in September 1933.

three-year research project that also included an extended stay in the New Guinea village where Margaret and Gregory had first met.

The work done by Mead and Bateson in Bali was probably more important for the methods they employed than for the conclusions they reached. Other anthropologists had used the camera as a research tool. But no one had ever used snapshots and movies to make such a rich, full record of a culture. One of their films was released in 1952 as *Trance and Dance in Bali.*

MEAD BECOMES A MOTHER

The approach of **World War II** made further research in the Pacific too dangerous. Mead and Bateson returned to the United States in 1939. In May, Mead learned she was pregnant, and

on December 8, she gave birth to her first and only child—Mary Catherine Bateson, a healthy baby girl. The name Mary was in honor of one of Bateson's aunts; the name Catherine recalled Mead's "lost little sister," who had died when Margaret was five years old.

The Food and Agriculture Organization of the United Nations chose Mead to receive its Ceres Medal in the mid-1970s. The medal, which is named for the Roman goddess of agriculture, is given to women who have contributed to the fight against hunger and helped to improve the lives of women and children. Above is a portrait of Mead on the 1975 medal. To the right, the anthropologist receives the award from FAO officials.

Who's Counting?

Just about all of Margaret Mead's writings and a huge number of items she collected during her fieldwork are housed in the Library of Congress in Washington, D.C. The library's holdings include about 1,800 boxes of her photographs, diaries, letters, and other writings. In addition, there are over 500 movie reels and more than 1,000 audio-tape reels and cassettes. In all, the Mead collection holds more than half a million items. If you averaged only a minute on each one, without taking any time off to eat or sleep, you would need a whole year to get through them all.

Mead prepared for the great event with all the energy she might have brought to a field trip in Samoa or Bali. She showed the nurses exactly how she wanted the delivery to go by screening for them a movie of birthing practices in New Guinea. Margaret took the step—extremely rare in those days—of having a film made of Cathy's birth. In the middle of the filming, Margaret's labor had to be delayed so the woman running the camera could get a new light bulb.

Margaret saw Cathy not only as her beloved daughter but also as one of her most exciting research subjects. She experimented with the styles of bringing up a child she had observed among the Pacific Islanders and those she had experienced in her own childhood. As always, she saved everything. "When I wanted as a college student to discard a great stack of my childhood paintings," Cathy later wrote, "my mother told me I had no right to do so—that I had probably had the best-documented childhood in the United States."

Mead's only child, Mary Catherine Bateson, followed in her mother's footsteps and became an anthropologist.

Paging Dr. Spock!

Mead had picked up a great many ideas about breast-feeding and child rearing in the Pacific Islands, and she wanted to put some of those ideas into practice when her daughter was born. In 1939, most American doctors had very rigid ideas about how often babies should be fed, how long they should be left to cry, and how soon they needed to be put "on schedule." Margaret looked for a doctor who would take a more flexible approach, and she found one— Dr. Benjamin Spock. He was present at the birth of Mary Catherine Bateson and became her **pediatrician**.

After World War II, Dr. Spock published a detailed guide to baby and child care. His book became the most popular child-care manual ever written, selling more than 50 million copies. Like Mead, he began writing a regular monthly column for *Redbook* magazine in the early 1960s. He also became a leading opponent of U.S. involvement in the **Vietnam War**, which Mead also opposed.

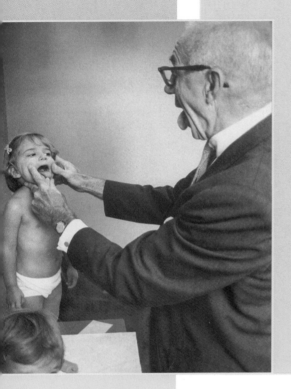

Dr. Benjamin Spock was present when Mead gave birth to Mary Catherine Bateson. By 1962, when this picture was taken, he was the world's best-known pediatrician.

PATRIOT

In her writings during the 1920s and 1930s, Mead had often been a critic of American society. When World War II broke out, however, she responded with patriotic fervor. This was not surprising. In Europe, the rise of Hitler's Germany—with its celebration of violence and racial hatred—threatened everything that she, Franz Boas, and Ruth Benedict cared deeply about. In the Pacific, Japanese expansion threatened to overwhelm the island peoples to whom she had devoted so much study.

Mead contributed to the war effort in several ways. At the urging of her friend Ruth Benedict, who had taken a job with the federal Office of War Information, Margaret went to Washington to serve as executive secretary of the Committee on Food Habits of the National Research Council. The idea was to keep up morale on the home front by making sure that people of different ethnic groups in the United States had the special foods their cultures required. She also worked to maintain morale by suggesting ways to suppress dangerous rumors that might lead to unnecessary worry or panic.

Some of her writings from the war years were collected in *And Keep Your Powder Dry: An Anthropologist Looks at America* (1942). In this book, Mead described what she thought were the best and worst aspects of the American national character. For example, she wrote that Americans are strongest when they feel "grown up and in control."

Mead (seated, second from right) took part in a 1940 conference in New York City on women's rights. Seated next to her, in the center, is First Lady Eleanor Roosevelt.

She thought the most effective strategy for defeating Germany and Japan was to organize the war effort in ways that put Americans' best personal qualities to their best use. One way government leaders could do this was by telling the truth to the American people, even when some of the news was bad. In the long run, she wrote, lying by the government would undercut morale, because Americans would become angry and mistrustful when they found out they had been misled.

CHAPTER 7

"MOTHER TO THE WORLD"

The end of World War II found Margaret Mead busier than ever. She was a mother, a scholar, and, increasingly, a figure of public renown. In addition, she still had her job at the American Museum of Natural History.

This bright picture was darkened by the passing of Ruth Benedict on September 17, 1948. Ruth's death of heart failure came as a painful loss to Margaret. She had remained at Ruth's bedside for five days as the older woman lay dying, and she wept openly at the funeral. After Ruth died, Mead took over her friend's job as director of Columbia University's program in Contemporary Cultures for four years.

Another devastating blow to Margaret was the breakup of her marriage to Gregory Bateson. "It was almost a principle of pure energy," Bateson said of his decision to leave his wife. "I couldn't keep up, and she couldn't stop. She was like a tugboat. She could sit down and write three thousand words by eleven o'clock in the morning, and spend the rest of the day working at the museum."

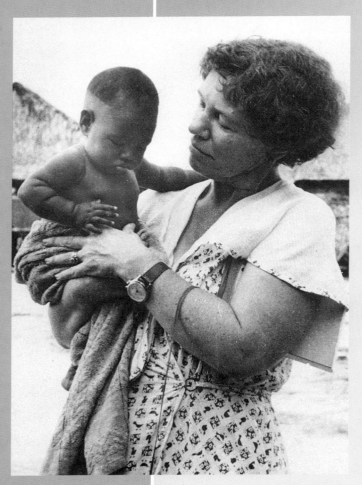

A quarter century after her first journey to Manus, in the Admiralty Islands, Mead paid a return visit in 1953.

This 1968 photo shows an aging Mead still hard at work. Adorning her desk is a decorated Tchambuli skull.

FLOWER CHILD WITH A WALKING STICK

While continuing to write and lecture at a dizzying pace, Mead made several visits in the 1950s and 1960s to the Pacific Island villages she had made famous through her research. She wanted to see how these villages had changed over the decades. She was astonished when she revisited Manus and people starting pulling out copies of her books and asking her about them. She found this experience very meaningful, as Mary Catherine Bateson related in a speech in 2001:

> *Suddenly there was an equation, a connection, that was to her terribly exciting, between those you study and those who study you. . . . It was one of the moments that made her really begin to think about a new kind of human unity. . . . I wish that she had a chance to meet the World Wide Web. She would have loved it.*

Margaret with a Manus mother and child. The anthropologist observed on her 1953 trip that Manus society was changing much more rapidly than when she first came to the village of Peré in 1928.

One scholar wrote recently that "Mead was the original flower child, interested in peace, justice, sexual freedom, and adventure." She may have been part

Generation Gap

Mead was responsible for the widespread use of the term "generation gap" to describe the huge difference in outlook and experience between those Americans born before World War II and those born after it. She gave lectures about the generation gap in the late 1960s. Her book on the topic, *Culture and Commitment: A Study of the Generation Gap*, appeared in 1970.

Today, the term "generation gap" is used to describe any large difference in values and attitudes between young people and their parents.

"flower child" in spirit. But by the 1960s—when *Time* magazine called her the "mother of the world"—the matronly Mead was no longer walking like the "small, determined eleven-year-old" of earlier decades. She had broken her right ankle in New York City in 1924, and she had broken it again in Manus five years later. After breaking the same ankle a third time in 1960, Mead began taking a tall, English-made walking stick almost everywhere she went.

Mead remained active well into her seventies and did not really slow down until her final illness

Margaret became a grandmother when her daughter gave birth in October 1969. "Grandparents need grandchildren to keep the changing world alive for them," Mead wrote in *Redbook* the following year.

Mead's Honors

Mead's remarkable accomplishments brought her many honors and awards. She received honorary degrees from more than two dozen universities. In 1975, she was elected president of one of the nation's foremost scientific societies, the American Association for the Advancement of Science. She was only the second woman to head the group, which was founded in 1848.

When she died in November 1978, world leaders such as United Nations Secretary General Kurt Waldheim and United States President Jimmy Carter paid tribute to her. Two months later, the Presidential Medal of Freedom—one of the highest honors the United States can bestow—was awarded in her memory.

In 1969, the YWCA in Philadelphia honored Mead and Princess Grace of Monaco for their contributions to justice, peace, and human needs.

in 1978. Her death from cancer in New York City on November 15 was headline news throughout the world. Her funeral at Saint Paul's Chapel, on the Columbia University campus, was one of many tributes.

The famous American social scientist with her English-made walking stick in 1975, three years before her death

It is normal for a scholar's fame to fade in the years following her death, but that has not happened in Margaret Mead's case. For one thing, the bruising attack on her work by Derek Freeman in 1983 had the unintended effect of keeping her name current. The one-hundredth anniversary of her birth in 2001 also helped to boost public awareness of her work. To mark the event, publishers brought out new editions of some of her best-known books. Her standing as a filmmaker, with Gregory Bateson, has also been helped by the Margaret Mead Film Festival, which is still held annually by the American Museum of Natural History.

In Her Own Words— Margaret Mead on the Future

Margaret Mead was a patriot and an optimist, but she was well aware of the challenges posed by a world in which peoples and nations are interrelated. This passage comes from an essay she published in 1965, thirteen years before her death.

Today every nation is faced by the same crucial problems: How to use its resources for the benefit of all its people; how to live at peace in the world; how to do its share in bringing the world's population into balance; how to make safe the air, the earth, and the waters of the earth for new generations; how to bring under control the powers of life and death that are now irreversibly in man's hands. . . .

As a people, it has taken us almost four centuries to weld ourselves into what is now—almost—a united nation. Much of what we have accomplished has come about through the pressures of the outside world. Strong, wealthy, and powerful, we must now . . . accept [our] responsibility . . . to the whole world, the only world in which we can act today and carry out our highest hopes for the future. We have no other.

TIMELINE

1901	Margaret Mead is born December 16 in Philadelphia
1922	Takes first anthropology course with Franz Boas and Ruth Benedict
1923	Earns bachelor's degree from Barnard College in New York City; marries Luther Sheeleigh Cressman
1925	Earns master's degree from Columbia University; begins field-work studying adolescents in American Samoa
1926	Starts job as a curator at American Museum of Natural History, specializing in the Pacific Islands
1928	Publishes *Coming of Age in Samoa*, which becomes a surprise best-seller; divorces Cressman and marries Reo Fortune
1929	Earns doctoral degree from Columbia University
1930	Publishes *Growing Up in New Guinea*
1935	Publishes *Sex and Temperament in Three Primitive Societies;* divorces Reo Fortune
1936	Marries Gregory Bateson; begins three years of fieldwork in Bali, Indonesia, and New Guinea
1939	Mead's only child, Mary Catherine Bateson, is born December 8
1942	Publishes *And Keep Your Powder Dry*; takes job on the Committee on Food Habits during World War II
1948	Ruth Benedict dies September 17; Mead succeeds her as director of Columbia University's program in Contemporary Cultures
1950	Divorces Gregory Bateson
1961	Begins writing a column for *Redbook* magazine
1970	Publishes *Culture and Commitment: A Study of the Generation Gap*
1975	Elected president of the American Association for the Advancement of Science
1978	Dies November 15 in New York City
1979	Awarded Presidential Medal of Freedom

adolescence: the period of time during which a person changes from a child into an adult.

anthropology: the scientific study of the origins, behavior, and development of human beings. Physical anthropology deals with how human beings have evolved and adapted to cope with their physical surroundings. Cultural anthropology emphasizes close observation of language, culture, and customs in order to show how different societies develop.

Civil War: a war (1861–65) between the Union (northern states) and the Confederacy (southern states). Slavery in the southern states was a major cause of the conflict, which was won by the Union.

curator: the person in charge of all or part of a museum's collection.

economist: a social scientist who studies the production, distribution, and consumption of goods and services.

fiancé: a man to whom a woman is engaged.

fieldwork: research done through direct contact with people in their own country or village.

impetuous: tending to act on impulse.

mentor: a trusted teacher or guide.

pediatrician: a doctor who specializes in caring for children.

Polynesia: the region of the Pacific Ocean extending southward from Hawaii to New Zealand.

social scientist: someone who makes a factual and systematic study of human societies and social behavior.

Vietnam War: a military struggle in South Vietnam from 1959 to 1975.

World War II: the world conflict fought between 1939 and 1945. The Allies (including the United States, the Soviet Union, Britain, and France) defeated the Axis powers (including Germany, Italy, and Japan).

TO FIND OUT MORE

BOOKS

Dunford, Betty, and Reilly Ridgell. *Pacific Neighbors: The Islands of Micronesia, Melanesia, and Polynesia.* Honolulu: Bess Press, 1996.

Mark, Joan T. *Margaret Mead: Coming of Age in America (Oxford Portraits in Science).* New York: Oxford University Press, 1999.

Mead, Margaret. *Blackberry Winter: My Earlier Years.* New York: Kodansha, 1995 (orig. 1972).

Mead, Margaret. *Letters from the Field, 1925–1975.* New York: HarperCollins/ Perennial, 2001 (orig. 1977).

Pollard, Michael. *Margaret Mead: Bringing World Cultures Together (Giants of Science).* Woodbridge, Conn.: Blackbirch Press, 1999.

Ziesk, Edra. *Margaret Mead: Anthropologist (American Women of Achievement).* New York: Chelsea House, 1990.

INTERNET SITES

American Samoa
http://www.amerikasamoa.com/
Learn about the land where Mead did her pioneering fieldwork.

Diane Rehm: Margaret Mead Special
http://www.wamu.org/mead/
Audio tribute to Mead from a Washington, D.C., public radio station.

Margaret Mead
http://www.amnh.org/exhibitions/expeditions/treasure_fossil/Treasures/Margaret_Mead/mead.html
Includes video showing Mead at the American Museum of Natural History's Hall of Pacific Peoples.

Margaret Mead Centennial
http://www.mead2001.org/
Site created to mark the 100th anniversary of Mead's birth.

Margaret Mead: Human Nature and the Power of Culture
http://www.loc.gov/exhibits/mead/
Exhibition put together by the Library of Congress.

INDEX *(continued)*

About the Author

Geoffrey M. Horn is a freelance writer and editor with a lifelong interest in politics and the arts. He is the author of books for young people and adults, and has contributed hundreds of articles to encyclopedias and other reference books, including *The World Almanac*. He graduated summa cum laude with a bachelor's degree in English literature from Columbia University, in New York City, and holds a master's degree with honors from St. John's College, Cambridge, England. He lives in southwestern Virginia, in the foothills of the Blue Ridge Mountains, with his wife, four cats (at last count), and one rambunctious collie. This book is dedicated to Jennifer and Michael.